Microsoft Project 2010 Essentials

Michelle N. Halsey

ISBN-10: 1-64004-127-3

ISBN-13: 978-1-64004-127-1

Silver City Publications & Training, L.L.C.
P.O. Box 1914
Nampa, ID 83653
https://www.silvercitypublications.com/shop/

Contents

Chapter 1 – Getting Started

Welcome to the Microsoft Project 2010 Essentials tutorial. Project is a sophisticated project management software that can help project managers with planning, assigning resources, tracking progress, managing budgets, and analyzing workloads for projects.

Research has consistently demonstrated that when clear goals are associated with learning, it occurs more easily and rapidly.

By the end of this tutorial, you should be able to:

- Open and close Project
- Understand the Interface
- Create a blank project
- Create a project from a template
- Open and close project files
- Add tasks to a project
- Set constraints on tasks
- Understand key terms
- View task information
- Sort and filter tasks
- Understand Task Indicators
- Split tasks
- Link and unlink tasks
- Create summary and sub tasks
- Create recurring tasks
- Understand resources
- Add and view resource information
- Assign resources to tasks
- Level resources
- Understand different task and resource views, including the Team Planner
- Use the Tools tabs and format the Timescale

- Create a baseline
- Update tasks and update the project
- Understand the Project Status date
- View the critical path
- Use change highlighting
- Create basic and visual reports
- Compare projects
- Check spelling
- Use the Page Setup Dialog
- Print a project
- Email a project
- Create a PDF of the project

Chapter 2 – Opening and Closing Project

In this chapter, you will learn to open and close Project and Project files. You will also explore the Project interface. Finally, you will learn to create a blank project and a project using a template.

Opening Project

Use the following procedure to open Project.

Step 1: Select Start (or press the Windows key on the keyboard) to open the Start menu.

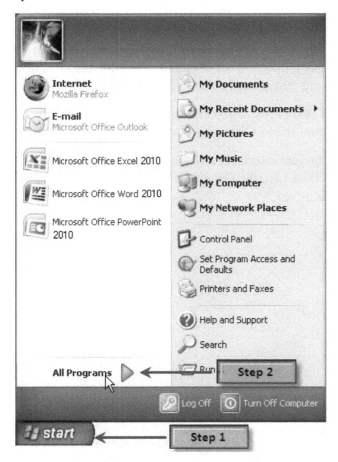

Step 2: Select All Programs.

Step 3: Highlight the Microsoft Office program group. Select Microsoft Project 2010.

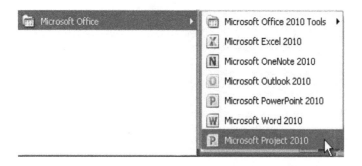

Understanding the Interface

Project 2010 has a new interface. Project 2010 uses the Ribbon interface that was introduced in Microsoft Office 2007 applications. Each Tab in the Ribbon contains many tools for working with your document. To display a different set of commands, click the tab name. Buttons are organized into groups according to their function.

In addition to the Tabs, Project 2010 also makes use of the Quick Access Toolbar from the MS Office 2007 applications.

Shown here is the Project interface, including the Ribbon, the Timeline area, the Task List, the Gantt chart, the Quick Access toolbar, and the Status bar.

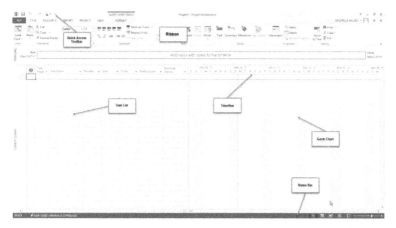

The Quick Access Toolbar appears at the top of the Project window and provides you with one-click shortcuts to commonly used functions. You may customize the contents of the toolbar by clicking the arrow icon immediately to the right of the toolbar.

By default, the Quick Access Toolbar contains buttons for Save, Undo and Redo.

To customize the toolbar, select the arrow next to the Quick Access Toolbar.

Add an item to the Quick Access Toolbar by selecting it from the list. You can remove an item by reopening the list and selecting the item again.

If you select More Commands, Project opens the Project Options window.

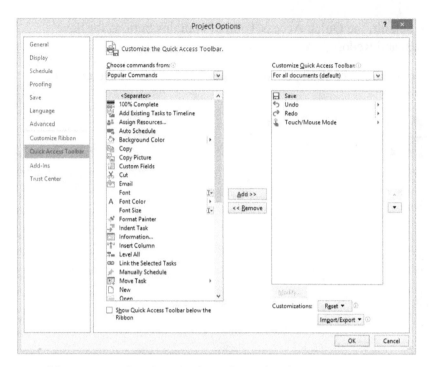

To add a command, select the item from the list on the left and select Add. Select Ok when you have finished.

Creating a Blank Project

Use the following procedure to create a blank project.

Step 1: Select the File tab.

Step 2: Select the New tab on the Backstage View.

Step 3: Select Blank Project.

Step 4: Select Create.

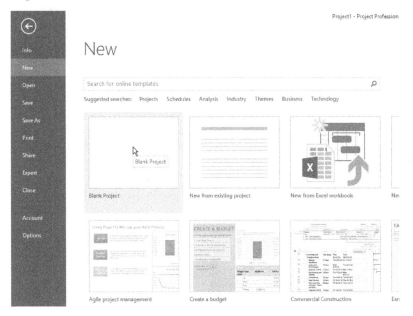

Creating a Project from a Template

Templates help to save time when creating a project. They can also provide consistency across several related projects. The New tab of the Backstage View provides links to several different templates. Some templates are created by Microsoft, while others are submitted by the community.

You can use or download these templates at any time. The new project can be modified to suit your needs.

Use the following procedure to create a blank project from an Office.com template.

Step 1: Select the File tab on the Ribbon.

Step 2: Select the New tab in the Backstage View.

Step 3: Select a template category.

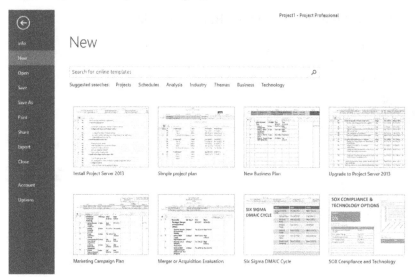

Step 4: Select a template.

Step 5: Select Create.

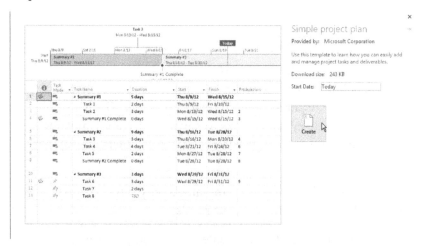

The Backstage view returns to the background after the new operation is complete.

Opening and Closing Files

To open a file in Project, use one of the following commands:

- The Open command on the Backstage View (on the File tab)

- Ctrl + O shortcut

To close a file in Project, use the Close command on the Backstage View or select the X in the top right hand corner.

Use the following procedure to open a file in Project.

Step 1: Select the File tab.

Step 2: Select Open.

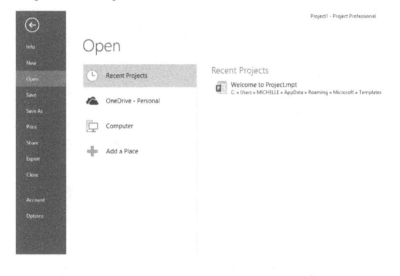

Step 3: The system opens the *Open* dialog box to allow you to locate the file on your computer.

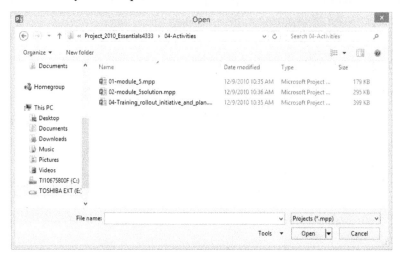

Step 4: Highlight the file you want to open and select Open.

Use the following procedure to close a file.

Step 1: There are two X icons at the top right hand corner. The top one is for closing Project. Click on the other X to close the current Project file without closing Project.

Closing Project

Use the following procedure to close Project from the Backstage View.

Step 1: Select the File tab on the Ribbon.

Step 2: Select the Exit command in the Backstage View.

Chapter 3 – Your First Project

In this chapter, you will get started using Microsoft Project by creating a basic project and setting up the project schedule. You will add tasks to your project and set constraints on those tasks to further customize your project.

Creating a Basic Project

The Project Information dialog box allows you to determine the start (or finish) date for your project to determine accurate scheduling.

Use the following procedure to schedule a project start date.

Step 1: Select the Project tab.

Step 2: Select Project Information.

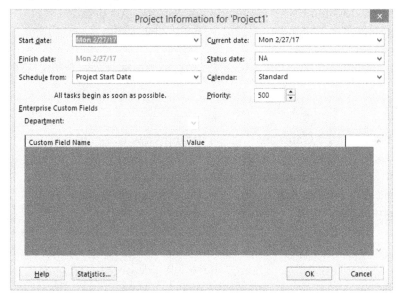

The system opens the *Project Information* dialog box.

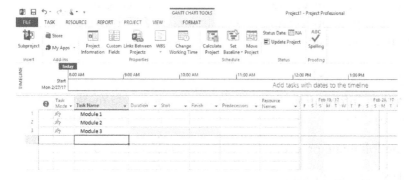

Step 3: Select the arrow next to Start date to choose a date from the calendar.

While you have the *Project Information* dialog box open, discuss some of the other options. You can select Project Finish Date for Schedule from and choose the date you would like the project finished instead. The Current Date and Status Date allow you to change the viewpoint when reviewing or reporting on details about your project. The Calendar sets the default calendar for determining the schedule.

Step 4: Select Ok to set your schedule start date.

Adding Tasks to Your Project

The left side of the Gantt chart in the default view works like a spreadsheet. You enter each task on a new row. You can add as much or as little information about the task as you like to get started. You can enter the tasks manually or paste the information from another program (such as Word or an email message).

Use the following procedure to add tasks to a project.

Step 1: In the Task Name column on the left side of the Gantt chart, enter the name of the task and press Enter.

Step 2: Continue entering task names for as many tasks as you want to enter.

Use the following procedure to add tasks to a project by pasting.

Step 1: Copy the information from another program. In this example, text is taken from a Notebook file (.txt).

Step 2: Place your cursor in an empty row in the Task Name column.

Step 3: Select the Task tab from the Ribbon.

Step 4: Select Paste.

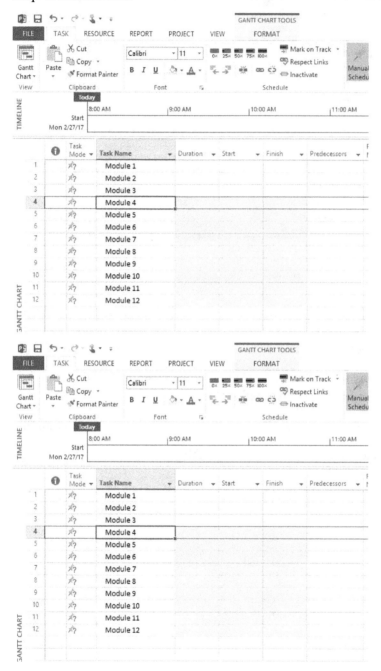

Setting Constraints on Tasks

The Task Details form is another way to enter task information. The form includes information on constraints. Constraints are restrictions set on the start or finish date of a task.

There are several types of constraints:

- As soon as possible

- As late as possible

- Finish no earlier than

- Finish no later than

- Must Finish On

- Must Start On

- Start No Earlier Than

- Start No Later Than

Use the following procedure to open the Task Details form and set a constraint type and date.

Step 1: Select the Display Task Details icon from the Task tab on the Ribbon. It is located in the Properties area.

nal

The system displays the *Task Details Form* in the bottom area of the screen.

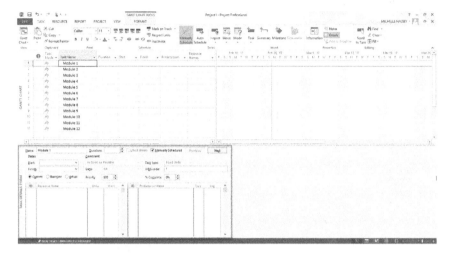

Step 1: You can use the Next or Previous buttons to select the task for which you want to set a constraint.

Step 2: Uncheck the Manually Scheduled box. Constraints are ignored for manually scheduled tasks.

Step 3: Select the Constraint type from the drop down list.

Step 4: Select the arrow next to the Constraint date and select the constraint date from the calendar.

Step 5: Select Ok.

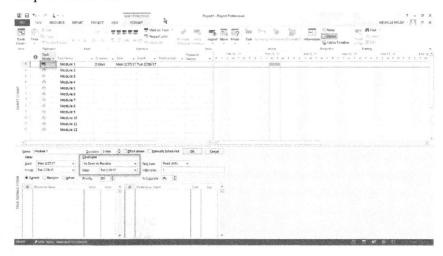

Chapter 4 – Adding Tasks

This chapter will delve a little deeper into understanding tasks. Project 2010 introduces manually scheduled tasks. You can also schedule tasks automatically using the Project scheduling engine. We will discuss the key terms for understanding tasks in this chapter. We will also learn how to view task information and sort and filter tasks. Finally, we will take a look at task indicators.

Understanding Key Terms

The key terms for understanding tasks in Project are:

Duration – is the amount of time a task will take to complete. When you are using manually scheduled tasks, you can enter anything that will help you schedule the tasks, such as "a couple of days" or "need to talk to Bob." For automatically scheduled tasks, you must put a number with a unit indicator, such as d for days, h for hours, or w for weeks.

Start Date – is when the project starts. For manually scheduled projects, this can be any text that will help you schedule tasks. For automatically scheduled tasks, it must be a date.

Finish Date – is when the project will be completed. For manually scheduled projects, this can be any text that will help you schedule tasks. For automatically scheduled tasks, it must be a date.

Resources – are the materials, people, and other costs associated with completing the project. Resources do not affect manually scheduled tasks, but do help Project to determine a schedule for automatically scheduled tasks.

Gantt Chart – the default view is the Gantt Chart. The right side of this view includes bars that represent the task duration.

Viewing Task Information

Use the following procedure to view task information on the *Task Information* dialog box.

Step 1: Select the task you want to view. You can select the number to the left to highlight the task.

Step 2: Select Information from the Task tab on the Ribbon.

ıal

Review the *Task Information* dialog box.

The *General* tab includes the following information:

- **Task Name** – the name of the task

- **Percent complete** – represents a percentage of how much of the task is complete

- **Schedule Mode** – select Manually or Auto

- **Duration** – indicates how long the task will take to complete

- **Estimated** – indicates that the selected duration is an estimate

- **Priority** – indicates a priority level in comparison with other tasks

- **Inactive** – makes the task inactive

- **Start** and **Finish** dates – indicates the start and finish date of the task, according to the indicated duration

- **Display on Timeline** – indicates that Project should display the task on the timeline

- **Hide Bar** – indicates that Project should hide the Gantt chart bar

- **Rollup** – indicates that Project should rollup the task with its summary task

Review the other tabs briefly.

The *Predecessors* tab allows you to work with linked tasks and task relationships.

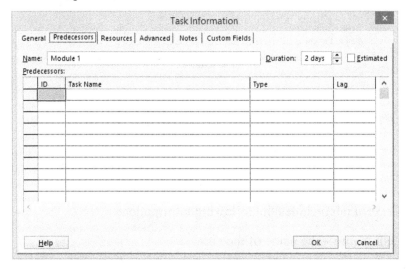

The *Resources* tab lists resources assigned to the task. We will talk about resources in Chapter six.

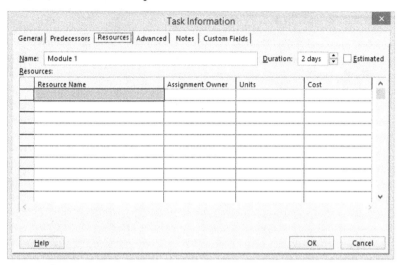

The *Advanced* tab allows you to set deadlines and constraints. It also includes the task type, WBS code (work breakdown structure) and the earned value method.

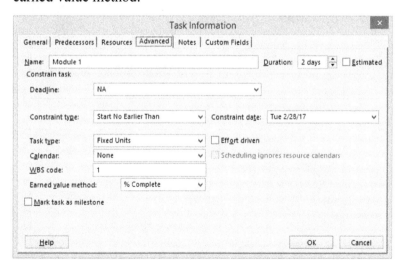

The *Notes* tab allows you to keep textual notes about the task.

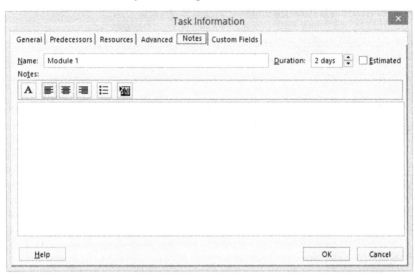

The *Custom Fields* tab allows you to include information in fields you have customized for the project.

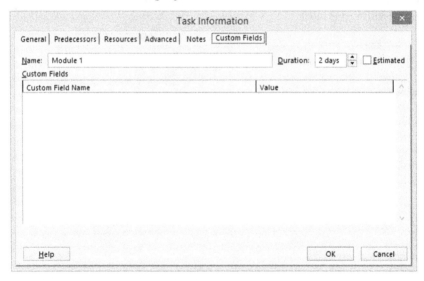

Sorting and Filtering Tasks

The View tab includes tools to sort and filter your task list. This can help you find a task in a long list of items, or filter the view to only include certain parts of the project.

Use the following procedure to see how to sort tasks.

Step 1: Select the View tab from the Ribbon.

Step 2: Select Sort.

Step 3: Select a sorting option.

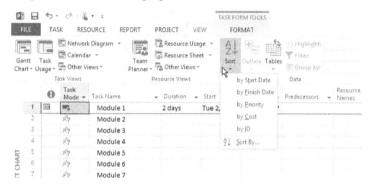

Use the following procedure to view the *Sort By* dialog box.

Step 1: Select the View tab from the Ribbon.

Step 2: Select Sort.

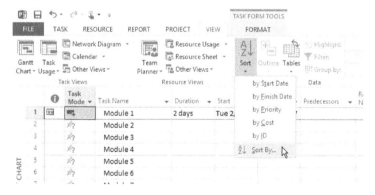

Step 3: Select Sort By.

Step 4: You can select up to three options for sorting, and determine whether they should be sorted ascending or descending. Select **Sort** when you have finished.

Understanding Task Indicators

The following list explains some of the indicators associated with tasks:

- Note Task

- Hyperlink Task

- Deadline Task

- Inflexible Constraint

- Flexible Constraint

- Recurring Task

- Complete Task

- Task Calendar

Indicators provide valuable information. Remember to check the indicator column to find out details about a task. Point out that other views include indicators as well, such as the Resource view. For some views, you may need to add the Indicator field to show this information.

Think of the indicators in the sample project file. When you hover over the indicator, Project displays a hint for the meaning of the indicator.

Chapter 5: Advanced Task Operations

In this chapter, you will learn some advanced techniques for working with tasks. You will learn how to split tasks to account for time away from a task. You will learn to link and unlink tasks, which can be used to create dependencies between tasks (such as when one task cannot begin until another is completed). This chapter also explains summary and sub tasks and how they can help you organize your project. Finally, you will learn how to create recurring tasks.

Splitting Tasks

You can split tasks to allow for time away from a task, such as when the resource needed for that task is temporarily reassigned to another task or has to take an unplanned leave. You can split tasks multiple times.

Use the following procedure to split tasks.

Step 1: In the Gantt chart view, select the bar for the task you want to split.

Step 2: Select the Split Tasks tool from the Task tab on the Ribbon.

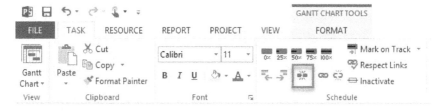

Project displays the *Split Tasks* dialog.

Step 3: Hover your mouse over the task. Project displays the corresponding date in the Split Tasks dialog.

Step 4: When the date corresponds to the date where you need to split the task, click the mouse.

Project inserts a break in the task, as illustrated below.

Step 5: You can drag the second part of the task to any start date.

The following illustration shows a task that has been split, and then resumed on the following Tuesday.

Linking and Unlinking Tasks

Linking tasks allows you to create dependencies between two or more tasks. To link tasks, select the tasks you want to link and use the Link tasks tool. To unlink the tasks, select the tasks and use the Unlink tasks tool.

Use the following procedure to link tasks.

Step 1: Select the tasks you want to link by highlighting them in the task list.

Step 2: Select the Link Tasks tool.

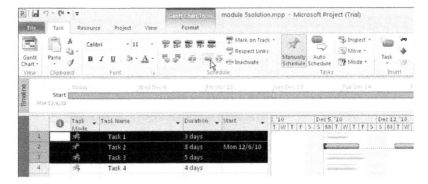

Notice the new start dates and the way the task duration bars on the Gantt chart have changed.

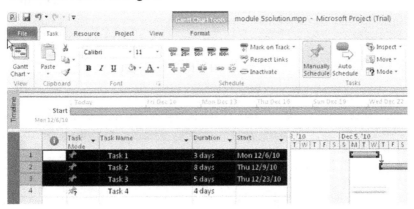

Use the following procedure to unlink tasks. Select the tasks you want to unlink by highlighting them in the task list.

Step 1: Select the Unlink Tasks tool.

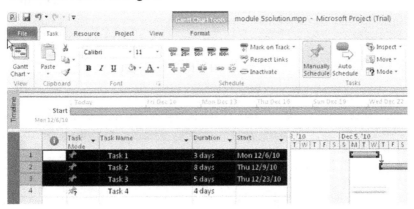

Creating Summary and Sub Tasks

Summary tasks allow you to see certain information about your project "rolled up" into one task that summarizes several related tasks. You can insert summary tasks or make existing tasks summary tasks. You can use the indent and outdent tools to make existing tasks summary tasks or subtasks.

Use the following procedure to insert a summary task.

Step 1: Place your cursor in the task that will be a subtask to the new summary task, or in a blank row on the task list.

Step 2: Select the Insert Summary Task tool from the Task tab on the Ribbon.

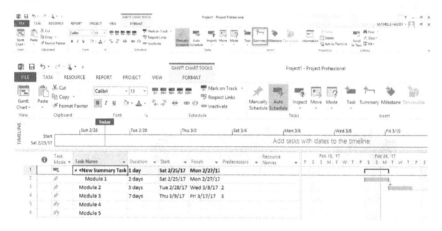

Step 3: Enter the name of the summary task.

Use the following procedure to make subtasks using the Indent tool.

Step 1: Highlight one or more tasks that will be subtasks to the summary task preceding them.

Step 2: Select the Indent tool.

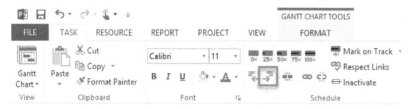

Creating Recurring Tasks

If you have a task that is repeated at regular intervals, it will save time to enter it as a recurring task. You enter the recurrence information when you insert the task.

Use the following procedure to create a recurring task.

Step 1: Place your cursor on the row below where you want the recurring task to appear in the task list.

Step 2: Select Task from the Task tab on the Ribbon.

Step 3: Select Recurring Task.

Step 4: Enter the Task Name.

Step 5: Select the Recurrence Pattern and enter the pattern details according to your selection.

Step 6: Enter the Start and End information for the Range of Recurrence.

Step 7: Select the Calendar for the task.

Step 8: Select OK.

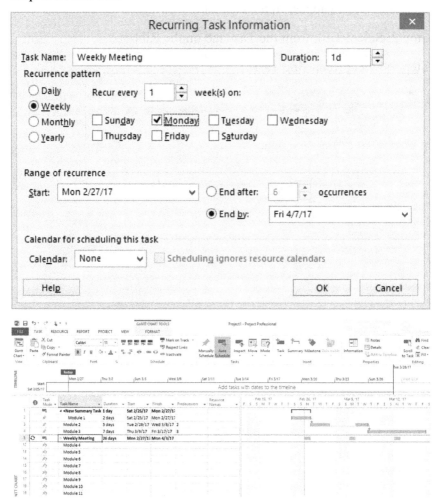

Chapter 6 – Adding Resources

This chapter introduces resources. Resources are the people, equipment, and materials needed to complete your project. This chapter will give an overview of how resources are used in Project 2010. You will learn how to add resources and view resource information. You will also learn how to assign resources to tasks. Finally, this chapter presents an introduction to leveling resources, which is a way to reschedule tasks so that your resources are not over scheduled.

Understanding Resources

The resources must be added to the project before they are available to assign to tasks. There are three different types of resources in Project 2010:

Work resources are the people included in your project plan. These are the people who will do the work of completing tasks related to the project.

Material resources are the items that are required to complete your project that are measured in units rather than work hours, such as cases of roofing shingles or gallons of paint.

Cost resources are fixed costs associated with your project, such as airfare or equipment rental.

Adding Resources

You will need to create your data base of resources before you can do anything else with your resource information. The Resource Sheet allows you to enter your resource information.

Use the following procedure to enter resources.

Step 1: Select the View tab from the Ribbon.

Step 2: Select Resource Sheet.

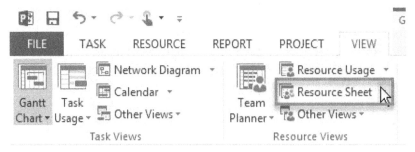

Step 3: Select the Resource tab from the Ribbon.

Step 4: Select Add Resources.

Step 5: You can add resources from your Active Directory or your Outlook Address Book. Or select **Work Resource, Material Resource, or** Cost Resource to add a resource of that type. You can also add a resource by entering information directly into the Resource sheet. Enter the Resource Name, the resource Type, and the Standard Rate for the resource in the Resource sheet. The standard rate can be indicated in different ways, including an hourly or annual rate for work resources and a per unit price for material resources.

Step 6: Make sure to save your work.

Viewing Resource Information

The *Resource Information* dialog box includes information about the resource, including availability and costs. You can also store notes about the resource and set up custom information.

Use the following procedure to view the *Resource Information* dialog box.

Step 1: Highlight the resource you want to view in the Resource Sheet.

Step 2: Select Information from the Resource tab on the Ribbon.

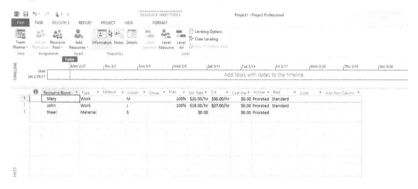

The General tab of the *Resource Information* dialog box includes basic information about the resource, including the name, email address, and resource type. Some more advanced options including the calendar and availability are also available on this tab.

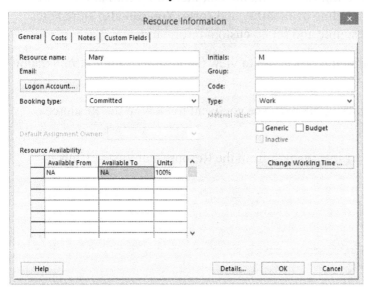

The Costs tab of the *Resource Information* dialog box includes information about the resource pay rates or costs.

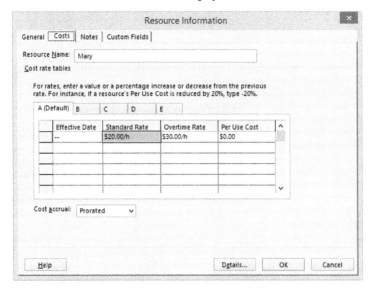

The Notes tab of the *Resource Information* dialog box allows you to include notes about the resource.

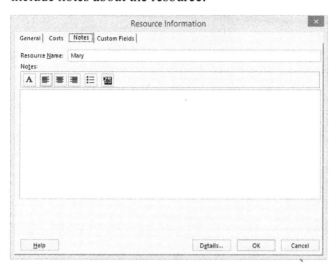

The Custom Field tab of the *Resource Information* dialog box allows you to add custom fields to the resource.

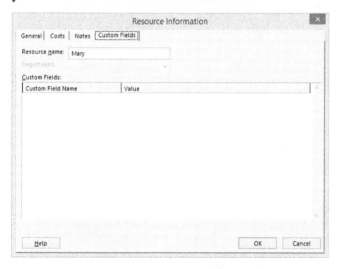

Assigning Resources to Tasks

Once you have added resources to your project, you can assign resources to your tasks. You return to the task view to assign resources to individual tasks. You can assign more than one resource to each task.

Use the following procedure to assign a resource to a task.

Step 1: Select Gantt Chart to return to the Gantt Chart view.

Step 2: Select the Resource tab from the Ribbon.

Step 3: Select a task from the task list.

Step 4: Select Assign Resources.

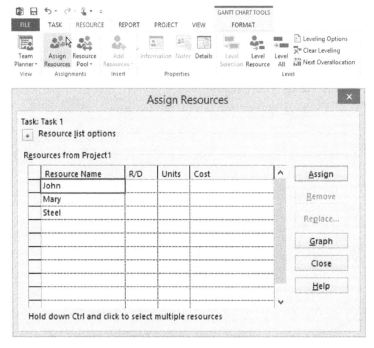

Step 5: Highlight one or more resources from the list. To select multiple resource, press the Shift or Ctrl key while selecting the resource name.

Step 6: Select Assign. You can also assign multiple resource individually by highlighting each resource and then clicking Assign.

Step 7: When you have finished assigning resources, select Close.

Notice the resource information has been added to the Gantt chart next to the duration bars.

Leveling Resources

The Level Resources tool in Project 2010 looks at task assignments for your resources and makes sure that a resource is not over-scheduled. If task assignments for a given day cause a resource to be over-scheduled, the affected tasks are rescheduled (sometimes by splitting or delaying tasks) so that the resource is not over allocated.

Use the following procedure to level resources.

Step 1: Select Level Resource from the Resource tab on the Ribbon.

Step 2: Select the Resource you want to level.

Step 3: Select Level Now.

Notice how Task 2 has been split to accommodate Joe's time at the Weekly meeting.

Chapter 7 – Other Ways to View Project Information

In this chapter, we will investigate some of the other ways to view information about your project in Project 2010. First, we will look at a new feature in Project 2010: the Team Planner. We will look at the important task views and the important resource views. You will learn how about formatting your view to get it to look just like you want. Finally, we will look at how to format the Timescale.

The Team Planner

The Team Planner is a new feature in Project 2010 that allows you to quickly see your resource task assignments, as well as unassigned tasks and resources that are free. You can drag and drop tasks to quickly reassign them.

The Team Planner shows the resources in your project, with bars to represent the tasks to which they have been assigned. The bottom of the view allows you to easily spot tasks that do not yet have resources assigned. You can also see which resources are free.

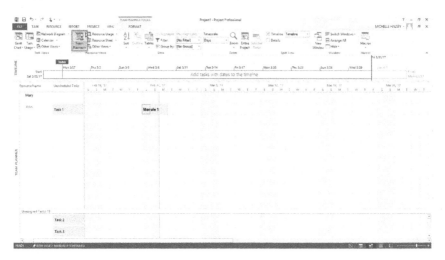

Practice dragging task assignments to new dates or resources.

Important Task Views

The Task Views area of the View tab on the Ribbon includes tools for the most common task views. You can also access other task views.

Shown here is the different task views available from the View tab.

Step 1: The Gantt Chart is the default task view. There is also a Tracking Gantt available, which shows the percentage completion for the tasks, instead of the resources assigned.

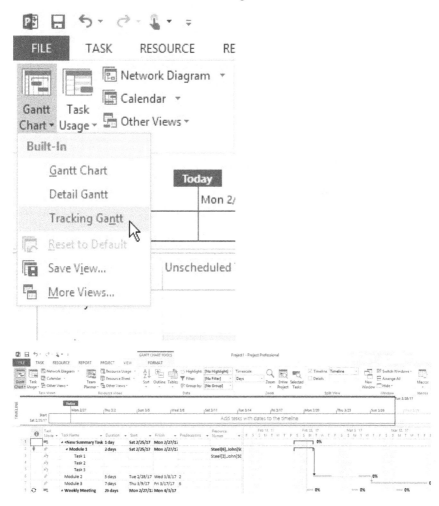

Step 2: The Task Usage view shows a chart of the work assigned for tasks.

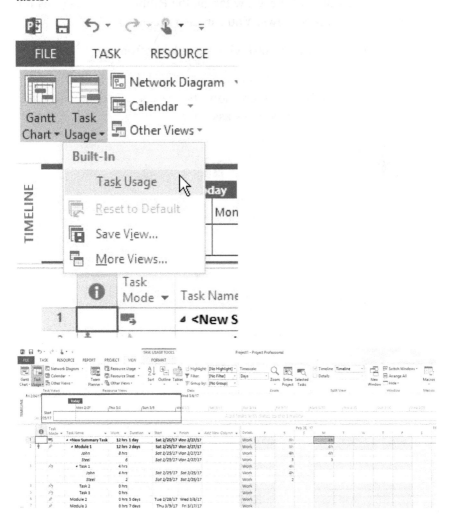

Step 3: Here is an example of the Network Diagram.

Step 4: Here is an example of the Calendar View.

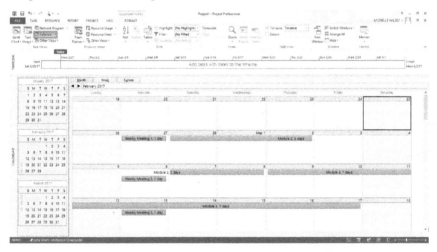

Step 5: Here is an example of the Task Form view.

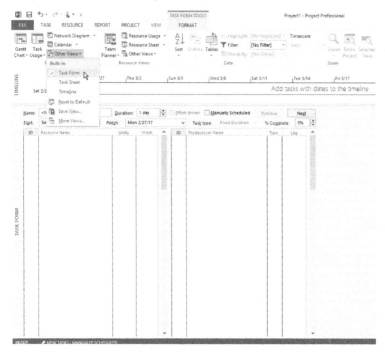

Use the following procedure to see the other task views.

Step 1: Select one of the Task Views tools.

Step 2: Select More Views.

Step 3: Select the view you want to use from the list and select Apply.

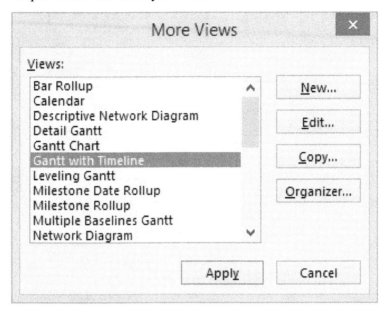

Important Resource Views

The Resource Views area of the View tab on the Ribbon includes tools for the most common resource views. The most important Resource Views are:

- The Team Planner

- The Resource Usage worksheet

- The Resource Sheet

- The Resource Form

- The Resource Graph

Shown here is the different resource views available from the Resource tab.

You have already seen the Team Planner and the Resource Sheet, where you add resources to your project.

The Resource Usage view shows a chart of the work assigned for resources.

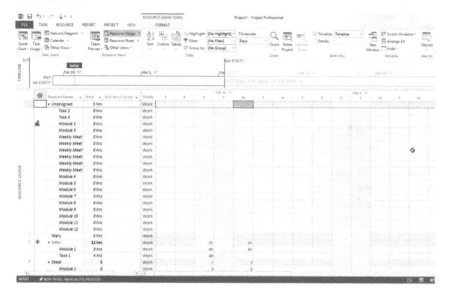

To access the Resource Form, select Other Views. Then select Resource Form.

To access the Resource Graph, select Other Views. Then select Resource Graph.

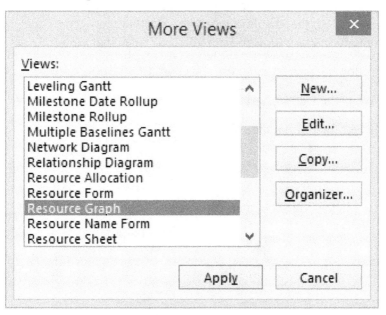

More Views

Views:

Leveling Gantt
Milestone Date Rollup
Milestone Rollup
Multiple Baselines Gantt
Network Diagram
Relationship Diagram
Resource Allocation
Resource Form
Resource Graph
Resource Name Form
Resource Sheet

New...

Edit...

Copy...

Organizer...

Apply

Cancel

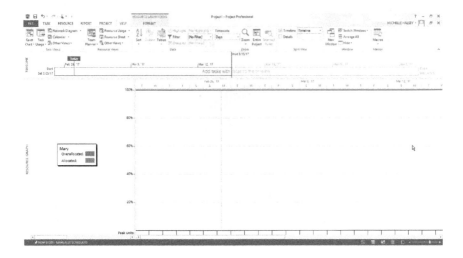

Using the Tools Tabs

Each task and resource view in Project 2010 includes a context-sensitive Tools tab that displays when you use that view. The Tools tabs include formatting tools to help you customize that view.

Use the following procedure to use the Gantt Chart Tools tab.

Step 1: Select the Gantt Chart view.

Step 2: Select the Format tab.

Shown here is the Team Planner Tools tab.

Shown here is the Task Usage Tools and the Resource Usage Tools tabs.

Shown here is the Calendar View Tools tab.

Shown here is the Task Form Tools tab.

Formatting the Timescale

The timescale shows the tasks in your project on a timeline. The timescale depends on how long your project and individual tasks take. You can view the timescale by different units of time to get a different view of your project. You can scale down to see the details for one task. Or you can zoom out to get a bigger picture view of your entire project.

Use the following procedure to change the timescale zoom.

Step 1: Select the Timescale dropdown list from the View tab on the Ribbon.

Step 2: Select a timescale option.

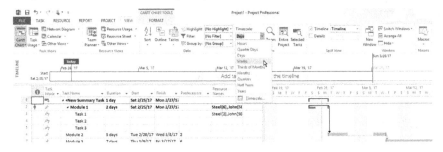

Chapter 8 – Managing Your Project Status

This chapter will help you learn how to manage your project status. First, you will learn how to set a baseline. Then you will learn two different ways for updating tasks. You will also learn how to update the entire project.

Creating a Baseline

A baseline plan allows you to evaluate your project's progress against that baseline at a later date. You can set several different baselines, giving each a different name so that you can manage the baselines.

Use the following procedure to set a baseline for selected tasks.

Step 1: Enter the tasks, durations, and other details of your base project before setting a baseline.

Step 2: To set a baseline for selected tasks, select the tasks you want to track from the Gantt chart view.

Step 3: Select the Project tab from the Ribbon.

Step 4: Select Set Baseline. Select Set Baseline.

Project displays the *Set Baseline* dialog box.

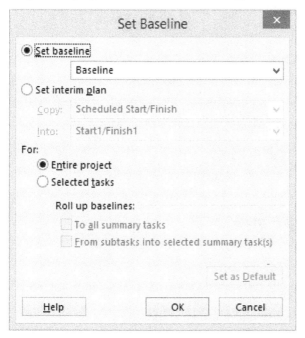

Step 5: From the Set baseline drop down list, select which baseline you want to set. You have the choice of the default baseline, or up to 10 other baselines, which are numbered 1 – 10.

Step 6: Select Selected tasks.

Step 7: Indicate how to roll up the baselines by checking the To all summary tasks box and/or the From subtasks into selected summary task(s) box.

Step 8: Select Ok.

The Baseline column stores the baseline information. Use the following procedure to add the Baseline column to see the baseline information.

Step 1: Right-click a column in the Gantt Chart view and select Insert Column from the context menu.

Step 2: Select a field to enter from the Field name drop down list. For each baseline you can set, you can enter the following columns to your table:

- Baseline Budget Costs

- Baseline Budget Work

- Baseline Cost

- Baseline Duration

- Baseline Finish

- Baseline Fixed Cost

- Baseline Fixed Cost Accrual

- Baseline Start

- Baseline Work

Step 3: Select Ok. Repeat to add more baseline information to your current view.

The selected baseline column(s) display the baseline values for the selected task(s). In the following example, the Baseline Estimated Duration column was added.

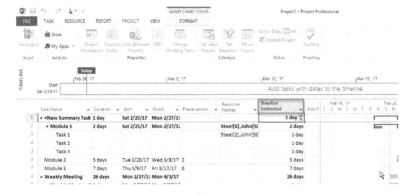

Updating Tasks

In order to report the status of a project, you must tell Project how much of the tasks have been completed. There are two ways to update tasks. You can use the tools in the Schedule area of the Task tab on the Ribbon. Or you can use the *Update Task* dialog box. When you have updated a task, the bars on the Gantt Chart include progress bars.

Use the following procedure to update a task using the Schedule tools on the Task tab of the Ribbon.

Step 1: Select the task(s) you want to update. You can hold the Shift key while selecting to select multiple consecutive tasks. You can hold the Ctrl key while selecting to select multiple non-consecutive tasks.

Step 2: Select the desired Percentage Complete tool from the Task tab on the Ribbon.

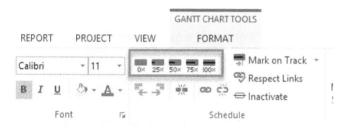

Use the following procedure to update a task using the *Update Tasks* dialog box.

Step 1: Select the task(s) you want to update. You can hold the Shift key while selecting to select multiple consecutive tasks. You can hold the Ctrl key while selecting to select multiple non-consecutive tasks.

Step 2: Select the Mark on Track tool from the Task tab on the Ribbon.

Step 3: Select Update Tasks.

In this example, multiple tasks have been selected.

Step 4: Enter (or use the up and down arrows) the % Complete for the selected task(s).

Step 5: Select Ok.

Here is an example where only one task was selected.

Notice the progress lines on the Gantt chart.

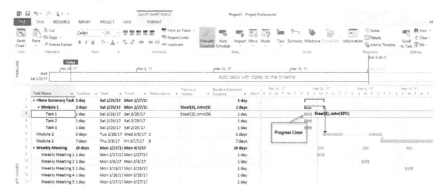

Updating the Project

The *Update Project* dialog box allows you to update work as complete through a selected date or to reschedule any uncompleted work to start after a selected date.

Use the following procedure to update the project. Select any tasks, if applicable, to update selected tasks.

Step 1: Select the Project tab from the Ribbon.

Step 2: Select Update Project.

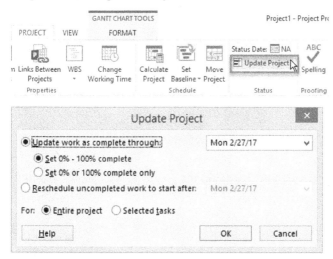

Step 3: Select the desired options and choose the date.

Step 4: Select Ok.

About the Project Status Date

The Project Status date allows you to view the project status and earned valued calculations. The Status Date defaults to the current date, but you can change the date, such as if you want to create reports on Monday for the status at the end of the day Friday.

Use the following procedure to change the status date.

Step 1: Select the Project tab from the Ribbon.

Step 2: Select Status Date.

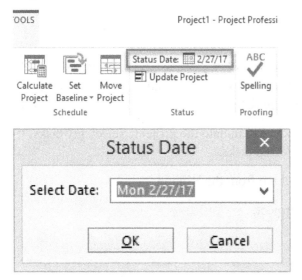

Step 3: Select a new date.

Step 4: Select Ok.

Chapter 9 – Updating and Tracking Your Progress

An important aspect of project management is checking on the project's progress and making adjustments in your plan where necessary. This chapter will explain first how to view the critical path. It will explain the use of change highlighting in Project 2010. You will also learn how to use the Task Inspector Pane.

Viewing the Critical Path

The critical path includes tasks that drive the completion date of your project. When there are many tasks in a project that includes task dependencies and other linked tasks, it may be difficult to determine which are the most critical tasks. Viewing the critical path can help the project management team make decisions about adding more resources to a project or changing the tasks in different ways to improve the critical path of the project.

Use the following procedure to view the critical path.

Step 1: Select the Gantt Chart Format Tools tab.

Step 2: Check the Critical Path box.

The tasks in the critical path are displayed in red.

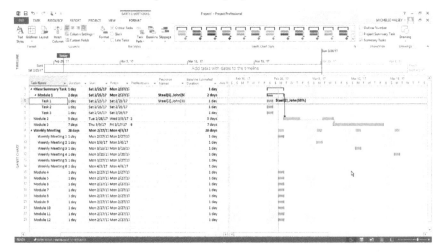

Use the following procedure to filter the task list to only include items in the critical path.

Step 1: Select the View tab from the Ribbon.

Step 2: Select the drop down arrow next to the Filter icon.

Step 3: Select Critical Path.

Project only displays the tasks that are part of the critical path.

Using Change Highlighting

During your project, you will inevitably need to make changes. Change highlighting can help you see how making changes to items affects the rest of your project.

Use the following procedure to view changed cells.

Step 1: Make a change in the sample file. In this example, the duration for one task was changed from 2 days to 1 day. Press Enter after making the change.

Step 2: Review the highlighted cells to see how the project has changed based on that change.

Use the following procedure to change the highlighting color.

Step 1: Select the Format tab from the Ribbon.

Step 2: Select Text Styles.

Step 3: Select Changed Cells from the Item to Change drop down list.

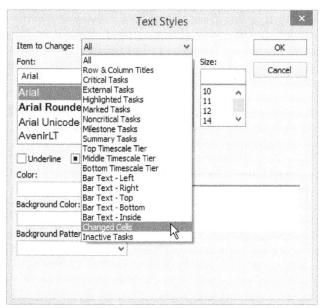

Step 4: Select the desired formatting.

Step 5: Select Ok.

Using the Task Inspector Pane

The Task Inspector Pane can help you track the timing and sequence of tasks. It can also show you how changes to one task affect the rest of the project.

Use the following procedure to display the Task Inspector Pane.

Step 1: Select the Task tab from the Ribbon.

Step 2: Select Inspect.

Project displays the Task Inspector pane on the left side of the screen. In this example, Project makes recommendations for improving the schedule. Click on the button to make the recommended change.

Chapter 10 – Creating Reports

In this chapter, you will learn how to work with reports. Project includes many different default reports, as well as visual reports that work with either Excel or Visio. This chapter will explain how to create basic and visual reports. You will also learn how to compare different versions of a project to see what has changed.

Creating Basic Reports

Project 2010 includes a number of basic reports. When you generate a report, you are taken to the Backstage View to preview or print the report.

Use the following procedure to open a report.

Step 1: Select the Project tab from the Ribbon.

Step 2: Select Reports.

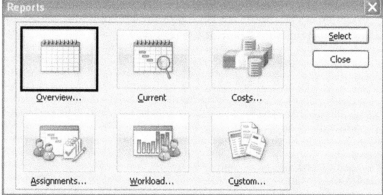

Step 3: Select Overview and choose the Select button.

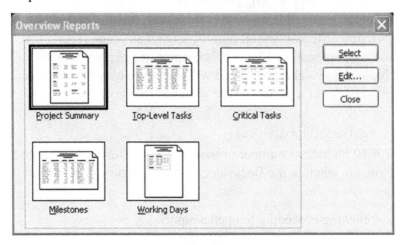

Step 4: Select Project Summary and choose the Select button.

Step 5: Some of the reports require a beginning date range. You would select it from the drop down calendar and select Ok. Then you would select the end date range from the drop down calendar and select Ok.

Project displays the report preview on the right side of the Backstage View. You can use the zoom tool (in the bottom right hand corner) to change the view. You can also print the report.

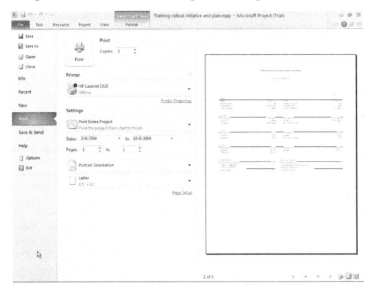

Creating a Visual Report

Project 2010 includes a number of visual reports. Visual reports work with either Excel or Visio, depending on the selected report.

Use the following procedure to open a visual report.

Step 1: Select the Project tab from the Ribbon.

Step 2: Select Visual Reports.

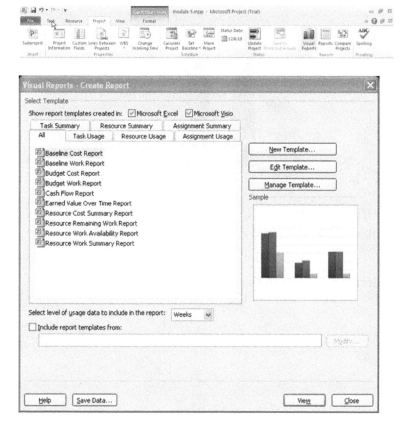

Step 3: For this example, select Resource Work Summary Report.

Step 4: Select View.

In this example, Project generates the selected report and displays the results as a Microsoft Excel Pivot Chart report.

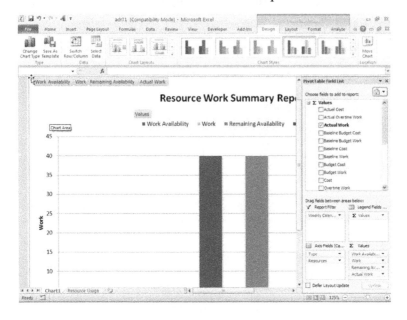

Comparing Projects

Use the following procedure to compare different versions of a project.

Step 1: Select the Project tab from the Ribbon.

Step 2: Select Compare Projects.

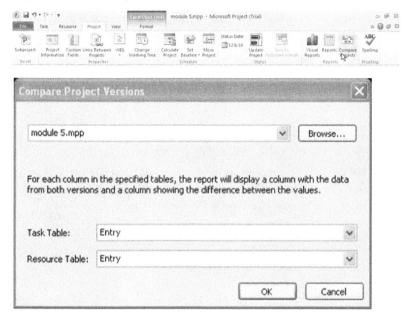

Step 3: If the file you want to use for comparison is open, select it from the drop down list. Otherwise, select Browse and locate the file on your computer.

Step 4: Select Ok.

Project displays a new project, which is the comparison report. It also displays both projects at the bottom of the screen. The left side of the Comparison Report includes information about differences between the projects.

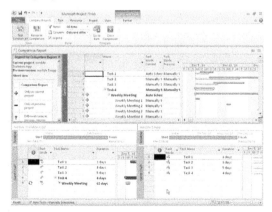

Chapter 11 – Adding the Finishing Touches

You can share your project with others in a few different ways. This chapter will help you prepare your project for other eyes by checking the spelling. You will learn how to use the Page Setup dialog box. Finally, you will learn how to print, e-mail, and create a PDF of your project to share with others.

Checking Your Spelling

It is important to check your spelling in your project so that you communicate clearly with other people who will read the project plan and schedule. The Project 2010 spell checker will find possible errors, suggest corrections, and show where the error is located.

Use the following procedure to check spelling.

Step 1: Select the Project tab from the Ribbon.

Step 2: Select Spelling.

Step 3: Project displays the *Spelling* dialog box with the first possible spelling error displayed.

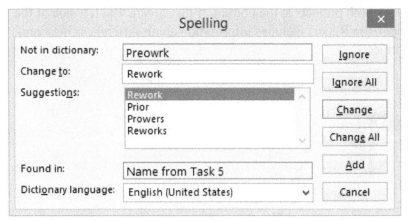

The buttons on the Spelling dialog box.

- The **Ignore** button allows you to keep the word as the current spelling, but only for the current location.

- The **Ignore All** button allows you to ignore the misspelling for the whole project.

- The **Change** button allows you to change the misspelled word to the highlighted choice in the **Suggestions** area. You can highlight any word in the **Suggestions** area and select **Change**.

- The **Change All** button allows you to notify Project to make this spelling correction any time it encounters this spelling error in this project.

- The **Add** button allows you to add the word to your dictionary for all Project files.

- The **Suggestions** area lists possible changes for the misspelling. There may be many choices, just one, or no choices, based on Project's ability to match the error to other possibilities.

- The **Found in** area displays the location of the spelling error.

- The **Dictionary language** allows you to select which language to use for the spell check.

Using the Page Setup Dialog

The *Page Setup* dialog box has several tabs, depending on which type of view you are working with in Project.

Use the following procedure to open the *Page Setup* dialog box.

Step 1: Select the File tab from the Ribbon to open the Backstage View.

Step 2: Select Print.

Step 3: Select the Page Setup link.

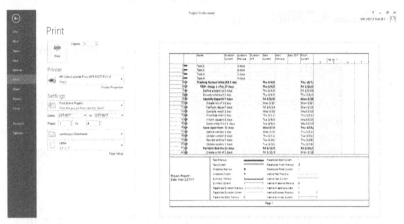

Here are the *Page Setup* dialog box tab for the default view – Gantt Chart. The *Page* tab includes the orientation, an option to scale, the paper size, and options for printing.

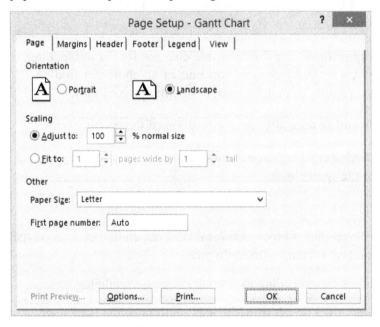

The *Margins* tab includes options for setting the page margins.

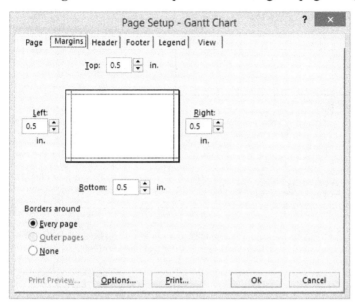

The Header and Footer tabs allows you to create headers and footers on the document.

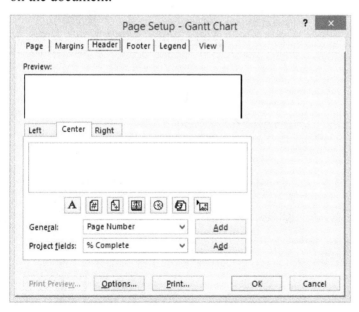

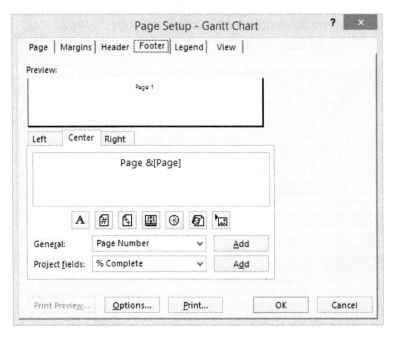

The *Legend* tab allows you to include Legend information for the project.

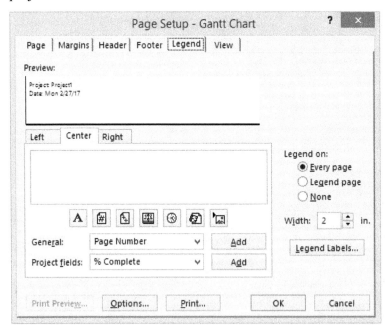

The *View* tab allows you to include additional information in the page setup.

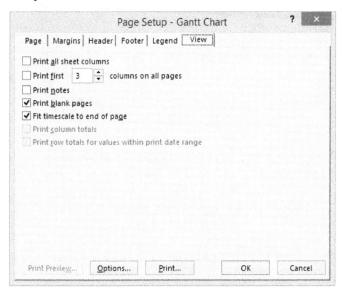

Printing a Project

The new Project 2010 Print tab in the Backstage View allows you to easily set your printing options and print your project.

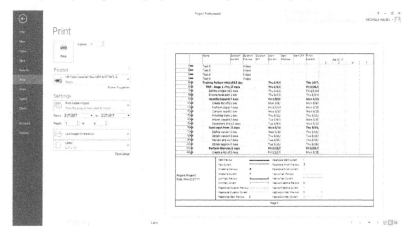

The buttons on the Print tab of the Backstage View.

- The **PRINT** button allows you to print the document using the current settings.

- The **COPIES** field allows you to print one or more copies of the project.

- The **PRINTER** allows you to select a different printer. The printer properties allows you to set the properties for that printer.

- The **SETTINGS** tool allows you to select different pages of your project or different dates.

- The **DATES** field allows you to select a date range to include in the print out.

- The **PAGES** field allows you to specify a custom page range to print.

- The other **SETTINGS** control additional settings for print, including the orientation and the paper size.

- There is also a link to the **PAGE SETUP** dialog box.

E-mailing a Project

The new Project 2010 Share tab in the Backstage View allows you to easily send the current project using your default email application. You can send it as an attachment or you can send a link to the file.

Use the following procedure to email a project file.

Step 1: Select the File tab on the Ribbon.

Step 2: Select the Save & Send tab in the Backstage View.

Step 3: Select Send as Attachment under Save & Send.

Step 4: Select Send as Attachment.

Creating a PDF

The new Project 2010 Share tab in the Backstage View allows you to easily convert the project to a PDF file for sharing with viewers who do not have Project installed on their computers.

Use the following procedure to save a project file as a PDF file.

Step 1: Select the File tab on the Ribbon.

Step 2: Select the Save & Send tab in the Backstage View.

Step 3: Select Create PDF/XPS under Save & Send.

Step 4: Select Create PDF/XPS.

Step 5: Indicate where to save the file on your computer and select OK.

Additional Titles

The Technical Skill Builder series of books covers a variety of technical application skills. For the availability of titles please see https://www.silvercitypublications.com/shop/. Note the Master Class volume contains the Essentials, Advanced, and Expert (when available) editions.

Current Titles

Microsoft Excel 2013 Essentials

Microsoft Excel 2013 Advanced

Microsoft Excel 2013 Expert

Microsoft Excel 2013 Master Class

Microsoft Word 2013 Essentials

Microsoft Word 2013 Advanced

Microsoft Word 2013 Expert

Microsoft Word 2013 Master Class

Microsoft Project 2010 Essentials

Microsoft Project 2010 Advanced

Microsoft Project 2010 Expert

Microsoft Project 2010 Master Class

Microsoft Visio 2010 Essentials

Microsoft Visio 2010 Advanced

Microsoft Visio 2010 Master Class

Coming Soon

Microsoft Access 2013 Essentials

Microsoft Access 2013 Advanced

Microsoft Access 2013 Expert

Microsoft Access 2013 Master Class

Microsoft PowerPoint 2013 Essentials

Microsoft PowerPoint 2013 Advanced

Microsoft PowerPoint 2013 Expert

Microsoft PowerPoint 2013 Master Class

Microsoft Outlook 2013 Essentials

Microsoft Outlook 2013 Advanced

Microsoft Outlook 2013 Expert

Microsoft Outlook 2013 Master Class

Microsoft Publisher 2013 Essentials

Microsoft Publisher 2013 Advanced

Microsoft Publisher 2013 Master Class

Windows 7 Essentials

Windows 8 Essentials

www.ingramcontent.com/pod-product-compliance
Lightning Source LLC
Chambersburg PA
CBHW071551080326
40690CB00056B/1796